Paleo Diet For Beginners

Top 30 Paleo Snack Recipes Revealed!

The Blokehead

About Us

The Blokehead is an extensive series of instructional/how to books which are intended to present quick and easy to use guides for readers new to the various topics covered.

The Series is divided into the following sub-series:

1. The Blokehead Success Series

2. The Blokehead Journals

3. The Blokehead Kids Series

We enjoy and welcome any feedback to make these series even more useful and entertaining for you.

Feel free to drop us a feedback on any of these websites:

Amazon
http://amazon.com/author/theblokehead

Facebook
https://www.facebook.com/theblokehead

Get Notice of Our New Releases Here!
http://eepurl.com/7tcHf

Like Us On Facebook
https://www.facebook.com/theblokehead

Table of Contents

Publisher Notes

Paperback Edition

Manufactured in the United States of America

Chapter 1
What Is Paleo Diet

The Paleolithic diet is sometimes referred to as the Caveman's diet, or the Hunter-Gatherer diet, the Stone Age diet and the Warrior diet. These days though, more people simply refer to this eating regimen as the Paleo diet. This follows the dietetic restrictions of our prehistoric ancestors, particularly the hunter-gatherers of old. This diet relies heavily on fresh produce, while shying away from processed food items that have proven time and time again to be detrimental to one's health.

It can be reasoned that, back in the Stone Age, health conditions like: cancer, diabetes, and tooth decay (among many others) were non-existent. People from that era, lived long lives and they certainly did not need to count calories in order to remain fit and healthy. It can also be reasoned that there were no documented accounts of overweight or obese populations from that era.

In other words, this is a diet that helps promote good health by simply eating good food.

Despite popular misconception, the Paleo diet is not a new fad at all. In fact, it is the basis of many modern day fad diets like: Atkins, baby food diet, cabbage soup diet, blood type diet, fruitarianism, Good Carbohydrate Revolution, high protein diet, liquid diet, morning banana diet, raw food diet, Scarsdale, South Beach, Sugar Busters, Zone diet, and the infamous Hollywood 48-Hour Miracle Diet (a.k.a. grapefruit diet.) However, unlike these aforementioned eating regimens, the Paleo diet does not encourage periodic starvation or the removal of solid food.

The Paleo diet was first suggested to the world in 1975, by a doctor named Water L. Voegtlin. He was a gastroenterologist who argued that the Paleolithic humans were carnivorous in nature. They devoured meat, and supplemented their diets with starches from fruits, nuts, seeds and vegetables. He used this as a basis for his successful treatments of gastric conditions like: abdominal angina, bowel obstruction, colitis, Crohn's disease, dyspepsia, gastritis,

GERD or gastro-esophageal reflux disease, indigestion, IBS or irritable bowel syndrome, peptic ulcer.

The good doctor also noted that his patients experienced:

• Gradual weight loss,

• Have higher energy levels,

• Have less acne and skin lesions,

• More stable blood pressure, and

• More stable blood sugar level, etc.

The Paleo diet is quite versatile. It follows certain guidelines as to what you can or cannot eat. But you also have the liberty to change this eating plan to suit your own personal dietary restrictions. For example: you can remove nuts from this diet if you have peanut or nut-based allergies. You can remove shellfish or other seafood items if you have religious or cultural restrictions against these. You can make this diet vegetarian or strictly vegan.

If you are new to this diet, you can follow this one simple guideline: if a cave-man does not have access to it, it should not be included in your meals.

Chapter 2
How Paleo Diet Works

To jumpstart your shift to the Paleolithic diet, the 7-Day Paleo Beginners Plan encourages you to clear your home of non-Paleo items that can tempt you to revert to your usual diet.

Keep in mind that the Paleo diet is more of a way of life than it is a dietary program. Making the right choices of food is the center point of this plan. Therefore, to make it easier for you to choose the right food, it helps that you remove unhealthy choices.

This will leave you to choose among Paleo food items and ingredients, and whatever you choose, you can be sure that they are healthy.

You will have seven days to train your body to start adapting to the Paleo lifestyle. Here is an overview of what you can expect during this period:

• You will be eating meals comprising of the following food items or ingredients: fresh fruits, vegetables, different types of meat, and seafood.

The above food items and ingredients are excellent sources of nutrients such as the following: fiber, phytochemicals, vitamins, antioxidants, omega 3 and healthy fats, protein, and low-glycemic carbohydrates.

• You will have to give up consuming dairy products and grains, including processed food. You will replace them with fruits and vegetables in unlimited quantity until you feel satiated. There is no need for you to count calories for your Paleo meals.

• Through the 7-day diet plan, you will be able to retrain your body to start eating food items attuned to your body's metabolism and genetic make-up.

As such, the diet can treat or prevent modern, autoimmune, and metabolic syndrome diseases including obesity, osteoporosis, cardiovascular, and Al zheimer's disease.

• You will be able to supply your body with healthy fats and protein from lean meat cuts. Contrary to popular belief, fats are necessary to improve the body's ability to burn fats naturally.

• You will develop the habit of choosing and consuming food in their natural state as much as possible. You will also learn to prefer meat coming from free-ranging or grass-eating animals instead of farm-raised animals whose meat still contain traces of chemicals and medicines.

Adopting the Paleo diet brings you multiple benefits such as but not limited to the following:

• Minimize your risk of autoimmune, heart, and degenerative diseases

• Lose your unnecessary weight healthily

• Clear your skin of disorders such as acne

• Increase your stamina for better performance

• Improve your sexual appetite

• Enhance the condition of your mind

• Enjoy healthier life

If you decide that you are ready to shift to the Paleo lifestyle, the best way to begin is through benefitting from the 7-Day Paleo Beginners Plan.

Chapter 3
Reasons Why Paleo Beginner's Plan Works

Burn your excess fat smartly with the 7-Day Paleo Beginners Plan. Unlike most plans that tell you what to do to lose weight, this plan will show you why you are having problems with your weight and how to resolve it in a long lasting way using the Paleo diet.

From here, you will learn why the Paleo diet works effectively in getting rid of your excess weight, and how it can get you going to achieve permanent weight loss results. This plan, especially designed for beginners, will serve not only as a guide, but also as a stimulator to start losing your weight.

What Paleo Diet Is According to Health Experts

The founder of the Paleo movement and the top expert on the Paleolithic diet plans, Dr. Loren Cordain describes it as the healthiest diet plan in the world. As the diet that originates from Stone Age ancestors, it works well with genetics to help you achieve your recommended weight healthily.

Nell Stephenson, who is a nutritional consultant and fitness trainer by profession and co-author of the Paleo Diet Cookbook, is herself a recipient of the nutritional benefits of the diet plan. The diet, according to Stephenson, involves eating the food that all the people during the Stone Age ate.

In brief, Paleo dieters follow these five (5) rules:

1. For each meal (breakfast, lunch, and dinner), you have to eat 2/3 vegetables plus your choice of fresh fruit, and 1/3 meat and fat.

2. You should get rid of inflammatory food from your meals. This includes all processed food, grains, dairy products, refined sugar, and legumes (beans, peanuts, lentils, and peas).

3. You can eat all you want until you are full without counting the calories.

4. No bread and cereal during breakfast, instead you should eat meat just as you would during dinner.

5. Cheat on your diet, eating three non-Paleo meals on a weekly basis.

The 7-Day Paleo Beginners Plan is your ultimate guide to start benefiting from the 2.5 million year-diet to achieve your recommended weight to stay healthy.

5 Reasons the Paleo Beginners Plan Works

There are several good reasons you will benefit from the 7-day Paleo Beginners Plan because it works. Here are the top reasons:

1. The plan kicks off by removing all temptations, which is certainly a lot easier than mustering your willpower to adapt immediately to the Paleo lifestyle.

2. It encourages you to rest and relax your body, the pre-requisite to start the diet plan. The plan works best when the body is free from stress.

A rested body will limit the production of Cortisol, the stress hormone that increases blood sugar for quick energy. This hormone also controls your mood and motivation among others.

3. The plan will show you tips and tricks on how you can choose the best Paleo food items and ingredients, how to cook and store your meals, as well as what nutrients you can gain from your meals.

4. You will not have to do things that will inconvenience you in enjoying your meals, such as counting calories. There is no need to count calories as long as all the ingredients comprising your meals are Paleo.

Hence, you can eat to your satisfaction without gaining extra weight, and while dropping your unnecessary pounds.

5. A natural diet activates and enhances your own body's ability to burn fats effectively and efficiently. You will start a dietary program where you will work with Mother Nature to stay fit and healthy.

Chapter 4
Foods That Can Be Included In Paleo Diet

To make following this diet easier to follow, here is a list as to what you can include in your Paleo diet.

Eggs

Organic and/or free-range eggs are acceptable, as eggs taken from the wild are very hard to come by. However, you can also choose commercially-produced eggs that are enriched with Omega-3 to maximize nutritional intake. Other egg products you can buy are those labeled with: cage-free, free roaming, or pasture-raised (pastured.) You can also buy from your local or nearby egg farmers to ensure freshness.

Aside from chicken eggs, you can also supplement your diet with quail and duck eggs. Other less conventional egg sources you can use are:

- Goose eggs

- Guinea fowl eggs

- Gull eggs (considered as a delicacy)

- Pheasant eggs.
To prevent excessive weight gain though, try to limit your portions to 1 to 2 servings of eggs per week.

Fish

Wild fish or fresh fish caught beyond the confinement of commercial fish pens is acceptable in the Paleo diet. Some farmed fish contain high levels of mercury and other heavy metal toxins that may be disadvantageous to anyone following this diet. If possible, always choose fresh fish cutlets, fillets, or steaks. You also cannot go wrong with buying whole fresh fish either.

You can include but not limit your diet to:

- Anchovies
- Atlantic cod
- Atlantic mackerel
- Bass (all kinds)
- Bluefish
- Catfish
- Flatfish
- Flounder
- Grouper
- Halibut
- Haddock
- Herring
- Marlin
- Monk fish
- Mullet
- Northern pike
- Ocean perch
- Orange roughy
- Pollock
- Red snapper
- Rock fish

- Salmon
- Sardines
- Shad
- Smelt
- Sole
- Swordfish
- Sunfish
- Tilapia
- Trout (all kinds)
- Tuna (all kinds)
- Walleye
- Whitefish

Fish roe (fish eggs with or without their sacs) is included in this list. These are usually high in both protein and Omega 3, but contain very little fat. If you are planning on including this in your diet, always use fresh roe, as opposed to brined, dried or pickled ones. The latter ones usually contain high levels of salt.

Caviar is a good example of brined fish eggs. You should eliminate this from your diet entirely.

The best one to add to your Paleo diet are fresh roe from:

- Alaska Pollock
- Black mackerel
- Bream
- Capelin
- Carp
- Cod
- Flathead mullet
- Flying fish
- Herring
- Illish fish
- Lump fish
- Paddle fish
- Pike
- Salmon
- Sardine
- Shad
- Smelt

- Sturgeon
- Swordfish
- Tuna

Fruits

Fresh fruits are always great additions to any diet, but try to limit portions of those that contain high levels of starch, sugar and fat (e.g. bananas and avocados, etc.) as these could entice you to gain weight.

Some of the best ones you should include in your diet (but do not limit yourself to) are:

- Apple
- Apricot
- Avocado*
- Banana*
- Berries (all kinds)
- Breadnut and jackfruit
- Caimito
- Cantaloupe
- Cherimoya and custard apples
- Cherries
- Coconuts*
- Durian* and Marang*
- Figs
- Grapefruit and Pomelo
- Grapes
- Guava
- Kiwi fruit
- Lemon
- Lime
- Lychee
- Mango*
- Mangosteen
- Melon (all kinds)
- Nectarine
- Orange (all kinds)
- Papaya
- Passion fruit
- Peach
- Pear

- Persimmon
- Pineapple
- Pomegranate
- Plum
- Rambutan
- Rhubarb
- Star fruit
- Tangerine
- Watermelon
* Use sparingly

Lean Meat

For the Paleo diet, it would be better to use organic grass-fed and not grain-fed meat. Always choose fresh cuts as opposed to processed or frozen ones.

Examples of common meat items are:

- Beef
- Lamb
- Pork
- Veal
- Venison

Other "exotic" or at least, less conventional meat sources are:
- Bison
- Caribou
- Elk
- Goat
- Hare
- Kangaroo
- Rabbit
- Reindeer
- Snake
- Turtle
- Wild boar

Organ meat is also listed in this category, such as:
- Beef bone marrow
- Beef liver
- Beef tongue

- Pork bone marrow
- Pork liver
- Sweetbreads
Mushrooms

All kinds of edible mushrooms can be used in the Paleo diet, just as long as you know how to prepare and cook these properly. It does not matter if these were cultivated or harvested in the wild. These usually have the same nutritional value and are not "polluted" with harmful fertilizers and pesticides. Use bottled, canned, dried, and fresh mushrooms for your recipes.

Avoid using processed mushroom-based products though, like: cream of mushrooms, soups with mushroom essence, and frozen pizza with mushroom toppings, etc. The mushrooms here are already devoid of nutrients and flavor.

Examples of edible mushrooms you can include in your diet are:

- Birch bolete
- Blewitt
- Button mushroom
- Buna-shimeji
- Caesar's mushroom
- Cauliflower mushroom
- Chanterelle
- Chicken fungus
- Crimini
- Coral fungus
- Dryad's saddle
- False morel
- Giant puffball
- Gypsy mushroom
- Hen of the woods
- Horn of plenty
- King oyster mushroom
- Matsutake
- Milk cap mushroom
- Morel
- Oyster mushroom
- Ox tongue mushroom
- Parasol mushroom
- Porcini

- Portobello or portobella
- Red-capped scaber stalk
- Saffron milk cap
- Shaggy mane
- Shiitake
- Snow puff mushroom or enoki
- Spike caps
- Straw mushroom
- Tooth fungus
- Urchin of the woods, and of course,
- Truffles (all kinds)

Using natural or real truffle oil is an acceptable substitute for fresh mushrooms. Always choose the ones that use olive oil, and not those with grapeseed oil. Clear oil is better than the cloudy ones, and green colored oil is better than the yellow. Make sure that the list of ingredients specify that the truffle oil contains actual truffle mushrooms.

Avoid the commercially-produced ones because these only contain synthetic substances that mimic the essence, flavor, and odor of real truffles. In other words, these have absolutely no mushrooms in them.

Mustard (as condiment)

You can incorporate this in your diet, because mustard is usually processed without additional flavorings or food additives. But there are some brands that sneak in a few ingredients that are not safe for the Paleo diet. If possible, buy only those labeled: gluten-free or organic.

If you find it difficult to remove condiments completely from your diet, substitute healthier alternatives like homemade:

- Atchara or atsara (pickled raw papaya)*
- Chipotle
- Chutney
- Cucumber or ginger pickles, including pickle relish*
- Guacamole
- Salsa
- Sauerkraut
- Vinaigrette
* Remove or lessen the sugar content, if possible.

You could also try substituting fresh produce for your usual condiments like: freshly sliced tomatoes, chilies, and onions. Freshly squeezed lime or lemon juice can be used as substitutes for commercial salad dressings.

Nuts and Seeds

These are actually great for snacks. You can consume commercially roasted nuts and seeds of any kind, as long as you do not have any allergies to these. Also, since the Paleo diet restricts salt, you may want to choose low-sodium products.

Roasted nuts and seeds would also make great additions to dishes and salads. To prevent unwanted weight gain, it would be best to limit your portions to 1 to 2 ounces per day. You can also buy raw nuts and seeds, and roast these on your own. This would help limit your salt intake.

Some of the most common types of roasted nuts and seeds you can incorporate into your diet are:

• Almonds
• Brazil nuts
• Cashew nuts
• Chestnuts
• Flax seeds
• Hazelnuts
• Macadamia nuts
• Pecans
• Pine nuts
• Pistachio nuts
• Pumpkin seeds
• Sesame seeds
• Sunflower seeds
• Walnuts
• Watermelon seeds

Poultry

It would be best to use organic fowl or poultry in your dishes, but you can also try cage-free, free-range, free roaming, pastured and pasture-raised birds. Some of the poultry meat you can safely include in your Paleo diet are:

- Chicken
- Duck
- Goose
- Turkey

Less conventional poultry meat you can use are:

- Emu
- Ostrich
- Pheasant
- Pigeon
- Quail

Chicken organs like gizzards and liver are also under this category.

Vegetables

There are a lot of vegetables that are best eaten raw, and they should be, as these contain the highest concentrations of vitamins and minerals. Tubers (e.g. potatoes and sweet potatoes) and some gourds (e.g. squash and pumpkin) should be included in the Paleo diet despite their high starch content. But you should limit your portions accordingly.

You can basically consume any vegetable-based dish you like, as long as these are not saturated in oil (e.g. diced vegetables smothered in butter or margarine, or salad greens smothered with ranch dressing.)
Some of the best vegetables to include in your diet (but do not limit yourself to) are:

- Artichoke
- Asparagus
- Beet tops
- Bitter melon or bitter gourd
- Bok choy
- Broccoli
- Brussels sprouts
- Cabbage
- Capers
- Cauliflower
- Celery
- Chayote

- Collard greens
- Courgette flowers
- Cucumber (all kinds)
- Dandelion
- Eggplant or aubergine
- Endive
- Ivy gourd
- Kale
- Lettuce (all kinds)
- Lotus root
- Mustard greens
- Napa cabbage
- Radicchio
- Spinach
- Squash blossoms
- Swiss chard
- Tomatoes
- Turnip greens
- Wheat grass

A number of gourds, root crops, and tubers should be part of your diet but these should be consumed as sparingly as possible, due to their high starch content. Examples of which include:

- Bamboo shoots
- Beet roots
- Carrots
- Cassava
- Corn (all kinds)
- Horseradish (including wasabi)
- Jicama
- Parsnip
- Potatoes
- Pumpkins
- Radishes, including daikon
- Rutabaga
- Squash (all kinds)
- Sweet potato
- Turnips
- Water chestnut
- Yam (all kinds, including taro)

- Zucchini (courgette)

You can also liberally use fresh or dried herbs and spices like:

- Allspice
- Annatto
- Anise
- Basil (all kinds)
- Bay leaves
- Caraway
- Cardamom
- Cinnamon
- Chicory
- Chili
- Cilantro
- Cloves
- Coriander
- Cumin
- Curry
- Dill
- Fennel (bulbs, roots, and seeds,)
- Fenugreek
- Garlic
- Ginger
- Jasmine
- Juniper berries
- Lavender
- Lemon balm
- Lemon grass
- Licorice
- Mace
- Marjoram
- Mint
- Mustard seeds
- Nutmeg
- Onions (all kinds)
- Oregano
- Pandan leaf
- Paprika
- Parsley
- Peppermint

- Peppers (all kinds)
- Rosemary
- Saffron
- Sage
- Sesame seeds and oil
- Star anise
- Sumac
- Tarragon
- Thyme
- Turmeric
- Vanilla
- Wasabi
- Wintergreen

Seafood

Almost all seafood items (aside from fish) are taken from the wild, or at least raised in pens that mimic their natural habitat. You can safely incorporate these in your diet, as long as you do not have any allergies towards these. Some of the best seafood you can use are:

- Abalone
- Clams
- Cockle
- Conch
- Crabs
- Craw fish
- Crayfish
- Cuttlefish
- Geoduck
- Lobsters
- Mussels
- Octopus
- Oysters
- Prawns
- Sea cucumber
- Sea snail
- Sea urchin
- Scallops

- Shrimps
- Squid

Roe (eggs and egg sac) from specific seafoods are under this category as well, like:

- Crab roe
- Lobster roe
- Prawn roe
- Sea urchin roe
- Shrimp roe

Edible sea weeds or sea vegetables are also included in this list. However, since fresh seaweed is very hard to come by, dried or dehydrated seaweed products can be used as substitutes. These are low in fat and contain very little calories. But some of these, like the common black nori, contain very little nutrients as well. If possible, always choose the fresh (or fresher) options, like:

- Beautiful fan weed, also known as (a.k.a.) Fried egg weed
- Berry wart cress
- Black scour weed, a.k.a. Landlady's wig
- Bladderwrack, a.k.a. Sea whistle
- Brown tuning fork weed, a.k.a. Brown forking weed
- Carrageen moss, a.k.a. Irish moss
- Clawed fork weed
- Cock's comb, a.k.a. red comb weed
- Coral beaches, a.k.a. coral stands
- Creep horn
- Creeping chain weed
- Dabberlocks, a.k.a. winged kelp
- Dead man's bootlaces
- Devonshire fan weed
- Dulse and False dulse
- Erect clublet
- Estuary Wrack, a.k.a. horned wrack
- Grape pip
- Kelp (e.g. Arame, Kombu, May weed, Sugar kelp, and Wakame)
- Hairy basket weed
- Harpoon weed
- Hook weed, a.k.a. Thread weed
- Iridescent Cartilage weed

- Mrs. Griffith's Little Flower
- Nori
- Oyster thief
- Peacock's tail
- Pink plates
- Pepper dulse, a.k.a. Royal fern weed
- Pod weed, a.k.a. sea oak
- Purple claw
- Sea grape
- Sea hedgehog, a.k.a. furbelows
- Sea horsetail
- Sea lettuce
- Sea petals, a.k.a. Broad leaf weed
- Shepherd's purse wart weed
- Slender cartilage weed
- Sponge weed
- Stalked leaf bearer
- Thong weed, a.k.a. button weed or sea spaghetti
- Wrack (e.g. Bushy berry wrack, Bushy rainbow wrack, Channeled wrack, Rainbow wrack, Serrated and Spiraled wrack)

Oils

The best ones are usually plant-based, but you can include fish oil in your Paleo diet. Fish oil can be acquired organically by simply consuming fatty fish meat like tuna and salmon. If you are not particularly keen on consuming these types of fishes, you can always include fish oil supplements in your diet. Just make sure that you ask your primary health care provider first if you can.

The list of Paleo safe oil includes:

- Almond oil
- Avocado oil*
- Canola oil
- Cashew oil
- Coconut oil*
- Grass-fed butter or butter substitute*
- Hazelnut oil
- Macadamia nut oil
- Non-dairy based butter or butter substitute*
- Palm oil*

- Pecan oil
- Pine nut oil
- Pumpkin seed oil
- Sunflower seed oil
- Walnut oil
* Use sparingly

Real truffle oil is included in this list.

Chapter 5
Food That Cannot Be Included In Paleo Diet

Alcohol

All alcoholic drinks are banned from the Paleo diet. This includes everything between beers and ciders, between distilled spirits and cocktails, between light ales and hard beverages. If you are using any type of alcohol in your desserts and cooked dishes, try to replace these with suitable ingredients like apple cider, white vinegar, or even grape juice.

Balsamic vinegar contains small amounts of alcohol. This should be removed from your diet as well. Other food items and drinks that contain alcohol should also be "banned" from your daily meals, like:

Alcohol-filled candies and confections, like:

• Black forest cakes
• A few chocolate candies
• Cherries jubilee
• Christmas cakes and fruit cakes
• Eggnog cakes
• Flambé desserts
• Rum cakes
• Tiramisu
• Whiskey pecan pies, etc.

Almond extract, vanilla extract, etc.

Any food or beverage that contains liqueurs, like:

• Chocolate liqueur
• Coffee liqueur
• Cream liqueur
• Fruit liqueur, etc.

Balsamic, malt and wine vinegar

Beer infused breads, cakes, and beer-based marinades, like:

• Beer focaccia
• Fish and chips
• Guinness cakes, etc.

Cooking wines

Port wine reductions in gravies, soups and sauces, like:

• Bearnaise
• Bordelaise, etc.

Rum or whiskey-based glazes (for baked or grilled meats, and cakes)

Wine flavored or infused cheeses and spreads

Candies and other Sweets

Candies and basically all kinds of sugar-based confections should be removed from your diet as well. These contain high levels of sugar, which in itself is already bad for your health. But any kind of sweet confection also includes gluten (from flour or other grains) and dairy products (usually from butter or milk.)

You should remove all forms of organic sweetening agents and artificial sweeteners from your diet too. These include...

Organic sweetening agents:

Agave nectar
Baker's special sugar
Barley malt syrup
Birch syrup (Xylitol)
Brown rice malt syrup

Brown sugar
• Dark brown sugar
• Free flowing sugar
• Light brown sugar
• Unwashed sugar

Cane sugar, and its byproducts like: juice and syrup

Caster or castor sugar,
• Bar sugar
• Berry sugar
• Super fine sugar
• Ultra-fine sugar
Coarse sugar
• Decorating sugar
• Pearls
• Sanding sugar
Coconut sugar

Confectioner's sugar, also called powdered sugar

Date sugar and its byproducts like: date paste, spread, or syrup

Fructose

Fruit sugar
• Pumpkin sugar
• Watermelon sugar

Glycerol

Honey and its byproducts like honeycombs, honey pellets, etc.
Jiaogulan
Licorice root
Maple sugar, syrup or taffy
Maltose
Molasses
Muscovado sugar
Palm sugar
Raw sugar
• Barbados sugar
• Demarara sugar
• Turbinado sugar

Stevia
Sucanat
Sugar beet syrup or sugar beet molasses
Sweet Cicely root
Sweet pine resin
Sweet sorghum syrup

Table sugar, also called granulated sugar and white sugar.
Sugar cubes
Sugar packets

Yacon syrup

Artificial sweeteners:
• Acesulfame potassium (Nutrinova)
• Aspartame (NutraSweet and Equal)
• Salt of Aspartame-Acesulfame (Twinsweet)
• Neotame (NutraSweet)
• Saccharin (Sweet'N Low)
• Sucralose (Kaltame and Splenda)

Colas, Energy Drinks and Commercial Fruit Juices

All colas, energy drinks, fruit juices, and basically any commercially-produced beverage should be removed from the Paleo diet. These are mostly sugar-based, and contain inordinately high levels of food additives and preservatives.

Commercially-Made Condiments, Jams, Marinades, Spreads, and Sauces

Certainly, the whole lot of these were not yet invented in the Paleolithic Age.

These days though, almost 99% of all condiments and jams are sugar-based, or at the very least, contain about 1 tablespoon of sugar per serving. Commercially-produced marinades, spreads and sauces have high amounts of glucose, food additives, preservatives, salt and sugar.

Some of the food items you should avoid are:

• Aioli sauce
• Barbecue marinade or sauce
• Bearnaise sauce
• Catsup or ketchup
• Chili jellies, sauce and spread
• Cocktail sauce*
• Curry sauce*
• Enchilada sauce*
• Fruit Preserves*
• Harissa
• Hoisin sauce
• Hollandaise sauce*
• Honey-mustard sauce
• Hot sauce or chili sauce
• Jams
• Jellies
• Marmite
• Mayonnaise
• Oyster sauce
• Plum sauce
• Salad dressings, including Italian and ranch dressings
• Steak sauce
• Sweet and sour sauce

- Tandoori paste marinade and/or grill sauce*
- Tartar sauce*
- Teriyaki sauce
- Thai peanut sauce
- Worcestershire sauce

* Homemade is better

Dairy products

All dairy-based products are considered disadvantageous to the Paleo diet, as these contain high levels of fat and salt. Many of these are also overly processed. Examples of which are all kinds of:

Butter and other dairy spreads, both organic and artificial

- Butter
- Ghee
- Margarine, etc.

Butterfat, buttermilk, and all products that contain these

Cheese
Coffee creamer, both organic and artificial
Cream and all products that contain creams
Curd, whey, and whey protein
Custard or any custard-based products
Fermented dairy products
- Sour cream
- Soured milk, etc.

Ice cream and gelato
Milk and its by-products milk skin

Yogurt and yogurt-based food products
- Greek yogurt
- Yogurt dips, etc.

Aside from cows, dairy products from these animals should also be avoided:
- Buffalo
- Camel
- Donkey

- Ewe
- Goat
- Horse
- Moose
- Reindeer
- Yak

Eggs

There are some types of eggs that are not beneficial to the Paleo diet. Although ostrich eggs are becoming mainstream and are usually harvested from free-range birds, you should avoid using these because of their high calorie content (2,000 calories in one egg.) Likewise, turkey eggs have extremely low nutritional value, but high in fat. Avoid these too.

Fish

Avoid all processed fish-based products like:
- Bottled or pickled fish meat
- Canned fish meat
- Caviar (brined or pickled fish eggs)
- Frozen fish meals
- Marinated fish fillets
- Ready-to-cook fish items (e.g. breaded fish fingers)

The meat used in these products are usually harvested from farmed fishes which may contain high levels of mercury and other heavy metal toxins. Worse, these might be an accumulation of fish byproducts and processed extensively to create cheaper food items. A very good example of this is frozen fish nuggets.

Grains

Grains are strictly prohibited in the Paleo diet. Some of the easiest ones you can remove from your daily eating regimen are:
- Breakfast cereals (and other cereal-based snack items)
- Amaranth
- Barley
- Buckwheat
- Bulgur
- Breads (all kinds, unless these are made from vegetables like sweet potato)

- Cookies
- Corn
- Crackers
- Millets
- Oats
- Pasta (all kinds, unless these are made from vegetables)
- Pastries
- Quinoa
- Rice (all kinds)
- Rye
- Sorghum
- Wheat

Aside from the alcoholic content, beer and malt are also grain-based, so these must be off the menu as well.

Although there are some controversies that surround the act of completely removing gluten from one's diet, it is still important to have a regular carbohydrate source. Carbohydrates produce glucose that is essential for maintaining the health of the brain. It is the one element that helps boost brain and cognitive functions. Without a regular supply of carbohydrates, your body becomes lethargic. You feel tired or exhausted all of the time. You also have a harder time thinking and focusing on anything.

In the long run, your internal organs suffer the most, particularly your brain, kidneys and gastric system, which could lead to numerous health issues down the line. To avoid all these, try to incorporate some starches into your meals. The best sources are from those that rank low in the Glycemic Index (GI) like: fresh fruits, lean meats, mixed nuts, starchy vegetables (e.g. sweet potato, etc.)

Legumes

These are simply the edible dry fruits from legume plants. All types of legumes are starchy and should not be used in the Paleo diet.

Examples of legumes are:
- Alfalfa sprouts
- American groundnut
- Black beans
- Black eyed peas

- Broad beans
- Chickpeas
- Common bean
- Fava beans
- Green beans
- Indian peas
- Kidney beans
- Lentils
- Lima beans
- Mesquite
- Mung beans (but not the sprouts)
- Navy beans
- Okra
- Peas
- Peanuts (and all peanut-based products like peanut butter)
- Pinto beans
- Red beans
- Snow peas
- String beans
- Sugar snap peas
- White beans

Meat

All processed meat items, particularly the ready-to-cook food items (e.g. microwavable meat-based snacks, or frozen meals,) commercially made dried foods (e.g. beef jerky or cured ham,) and canned meat (e.g. luncheon meat or Vienna sausages.) These are usually made from an accumulation of animal byproducts from multiple food production plants, then processed extensively with food additives and preservatives. The resulting "meat" is usually devoid of any nutritional value but has high levels of salt, sugar and other ingredients which are not good for the body.

Poultry

All processed poultry-based food items like breaded chicken fingers, chicken nuggets, marinated chicken pieces, etc. Should be off the menu.

Oils

Some may argue that beef lard and bacon grease should be included in Paleo safe oils because most vegetable oils were not yet created in the Paleolithic age. This may be so, but animal-based oils and rendered fats are incredibly high in saturated oi. When consumed regularly, these could cause all manner of health conditions, like: atherosclerosis, diabetes, heart disease, and stroke. At any rate, you certainly do not want to serve these to your kids.

Fish oil is acceptable though, as with high quality truffle oil.

Other oils you should avoid in the Paleo diet are:

• Any animal-based oils (except fish oils)
• Beech nut oil
• Bitter gourd oil
• Bottle gourd oil
• Butternut squash seed oil
• Cottonseed oil
• Corn oil
• Grapefruit seed oil
• Lemon oil
• Mustard seed oil
• Orange oil
• Peanut oil
• Pistachio oil
• Rapeseed oil
• Safflower oil
• Sesame oil
• Soybean oil
• Watermelon seed oil

Paleo diet also suggests that you remove all processed food and dairy products from your daily meals. This means that butter or margarine should be removed from the menu too.

Chapter 6
Paleo Snacks Recipes

Quick & Easy Kale Chips

Ingredients
• 1 bunch of kale, washed and dried
• 2 tbsp olive oil
• salt to taste

Directions
1. Preheat oven to 300 degrees. Remove the center stems and either tear or cut up the leaves.
2. Toss the kale and olive oil together in a large bowl; sprinkle with salt. Spread on a baking sheet (or two, depending on the amount of kale). Bake at 300 degrees for 15 minutes or until crisp.

Source: http://paleogrubs.com/kale-chips-recipe

Cucumber-Watermelon Sammies

Ingredients
- 2 medium cucumbers
- about 1/2 of a mini watermelon

Instructions
1. Use a vegetable peeler to remove the cucumber's dark green skin. Slice it into ½" thick circles and then trim the circles into 1" x 1" squares. We made a small amount, but you can keep making squares until you have what you need.
2. Slice the watermelon in half and create ½ thick slices. Out of each slice, cut out 1" x 1" squares.
3. Create the mini sandwiches by stacking cucumber, then watermelon, then cucumber. Spear each stack with a toothpick until you're all out of ingredients.

Source: http://thefitchen.com/2013/06/30/cucumber-watermelon-sandwiches/

Anti-Inflammies: A Healthy Gummy Snack

Ingredients
- 3/4 cup citrus juice, freshly squeezed*
- 3/4 cup all natural fruit juice, preferably freshly squeezed**
- 4 Tbsp. good quality gelatin (I use this brand here)
- 3 Tbsp. raw honey
- 1/4 tsp. ginger (freshly grated with a microplane or ground)
- 1/4 tsp. turmeric (freshly grated with a microplane or ground)

Notes:
* For a sour gummy use lemon or lime juice, for a sweeter, milder gummy use orange juice
** I used cherry juice because I had it on hand. You can juice your own fruit or use freshly squeezed juice from an orange. Just do not use pineapple juice. The enzymes will break down the gelatin.

Directions
1. In a small saucepan, whisk together citrus juice, fruit juice and gelatin until there are no lumps. Heat the liquid over low heat until liquid is warmed and gelatin is completely dissolved.

2. Remove from heat and stir in honey, ginger and turmeric with a spoon.
3. Pour liquid into a shape-molded ice/silicone tray (find it here) or pour it into a casserole dish*.
4. Refrigerate until liquid is set (at least 30 minutes).
5. Serve cold or at room temperature.

Notes:
*If you pour it into a casserole dish, pour a thin single layer. Once the liquid is set, cut the gummy snacks into bite-sized squares
**Per Mommypotamus, gummy snacks will last two weeks in the fridge.

Source: http://thesproutingseed.com/anti-inflammies-healthy-gummy-snack/

Wholefood Simply Snack Bars

Ingredients
• 1/2 cup almond butter*
• 1 cup (250 grams) cooled roast pumpkin or pumpkin puree
• 3 cups desiccated coconut (finely shredded dried coconut)
• 1 (150 grams) ripe banana
• 1 teaspoon cinnamon
• 1 teaspoon vanilla
• pinch of salt
*You can use half hulled tahini and half honey in place of the nut butter.

Directions

1. Preheat your oven to 175 Degrees Celcius or 350 Degrees Fahrenheit.
2. Grease and line a 20cm x 20cm square cake tin with baking paper hanging over the sides for easy removal.
3. Place all ingredients into your blender or food processor in the order listed, blend to combine.
4. Press the mixture into the tin and cook for 30 minutes or until golden on top and an inserted skewer comes out cleanly.
5. Remove from the oven, leave in the tin for five minutes then carefully move the slice onto a cooling rack. Once it has cooled chop into bars. Enjoy!

Source: http://www.wholefoodsimply.com/wholefood-simply-snack-bars/

Paleo Apple 'Nachos'

Ingredients
• apples
• fresh lemon juice
• almond butter
• chocolate chips
• unsweetened shredded coconut
• sliced almonds

Instructions
1. slice apples and toss with the lemon juice in a large bowl
2. arrange the apples in a plate and drizzle with almond butter. You can use a pastry/piping bag or a ziploc bag to drizzle the almond butter.
3. sprinkle with shredded coconut, chocolate chips and sliced almonds

Source:http://livinghealthywithchocolate.com/desserts/paleo-apple-na-chos-2715/

Low Carb Cajun Cauliflower Mini Dogs

Ingredients
• 12 mini sausages, I used Cajun spiced ones, but you could use plain or other kinds (make sure they are gluten free, nitrate free and low in carbs, 2 carbs or less per serving).
• 1 cup cauliflower, riced or ground in food processor.
• ¼ cup coconut flour.
• 2 eggs, beaten.
• ¼ cup grated cheese of choice, (I used cheddar) * Optional, can omit for dairy free.
• 1 ½ tbsp butter, melted or coconut oil, melted.
• ½ tsp baking soda + 1 tsp apple cider vinegar mixed in a separate pinch bowl (will be very fizzy).
• 1 tbsp red pepper sauce, I used Frank's Red pepper Sauce (you can use more or less red pepper sauce depending on your spicy meter, one tbsp. made a mild to medium spice level.) * optional.
• ½ tsp ground mustard powder.
• ¼ tsp smoked paprika, or paprika.
• ¼ tsp sea salt.
• ⅛ tsp chili powder.
• 1 to 2 tsp minced jalapeños or mild chilies *optional, only for spicy lovers.

Dipping Options:
• Organic mustard, (check ingredients for gluten) * optional.
• Favorite hot sauce, I used Frank's Red Pepper Sauce (make sure gluten free and low carb).

Instructions
1. Preheat oven to 400 F, and line a baking sheet with parchment paper or oil a baking sheet.
2. Put cauliflower florets into the food processor and process until rice texture forms, or can rice or grate it.
3. In large mixing bowl combine: cauliflower rice, coconut flour, eggs, optional cheese, butter or coconut oil, melted, red pepper sauce, ground mustard, paprika, sea salt, chili powder, optional minced jalapenos or chilies, and baking soda-vinegar mixture. Stir until thoroughly combined.
4. Place a small spoonful of cauliflower batter on the baking sheet, then smash flat with spoon. Repeat 12 times* as shown in photo above. Could skip this part for a faster prep, but there will be a small open spot at bottom of dog. I did a few each way and it worked out great.
5. Take mini sausages and press one dog into each battered section on the baking sheet *as shown in photo above.*
6. Place another spoonful of batter on top of each dog. Use fingers and hands to squish batter around and cover sausages,* as shown in photo above.*
7. Then I used the back of spoon to smooth a little, but they don't have to be pretty. Once sausages are covered and shaped, they can go into the preheated oven.
8. Bake for 23 minutes, or until top are somewhat firm, and browning.
9. Remove, cool, and serve with favorite dipping sauce, mustard, or hot sauce.

Source:http://www.beautyandthefoodie.com/low-carb-cajun-cauliflower-mini-dogs/

Energy Bars
(Makes about 5 bars)

Ingredients
• 1 medium, banana (very ripe works best)
• 1/4 cup nuts (I used salted cashews)
• 1/3 cup dried fruit (I used cherries)
• 1/4 cup seeds (I used sunflower seeds, or sub for more nuts)
• 1/4 cup vanilla protein powder (try with another flavor and let me know how it is)

- 2 tbsp arrowroot starch (or other starch)
- 1/2 cup almond flour (thought I should add parenthesis here too)

Directions
1. In a bowl, mash the banana well with a fork or other handy utensil. It doesn't have to be perfect.
2. Add almond flour and arrowroot starch and mix well.
3. Add in your mix-ins and stir well.
4. Grease a small pan (I used a meatloaf pan and it was perfect) with your favorite oil and pour mixture in, pressing down where needed to evenly distribute throughout.
5. Bake on around 275 for 30-40 minutes, or until the edges start to brown.
6. Take out the loaf, and cut into cute bars or squares.
7. Power up as needed! And store in the fridge after a day.

Source: http://www.livehealtheasy.com/2013/10/energy-bars-and-powering-through.html

Spiced Butternut Chips

Ingredients (makes 4 servings):
- 1 medium butternut squash (400g / 14.1 oz)
- 2 tbsp extra virgin coconut oil or ghee, melted
- 1 tsp gingerbread spice mix (~ ½ tsp cinnamon, pinch nutmeg, ginger, cloves and allspice)
- pinch salt (or more in case you don't use stevia and prefer the chips salty)
- Optional: 3-6 drops liquid Stevia extract (I recommend SweetLeaf or NuNaturals) or other healthy low-carb sweetener from this list

Notes: Oils that have high smoke points are suitable for cooking (butter, ghee, coconut oil, macadamia oil, etc.).
When looking for ingredients, try to get them in their most natural form (organic, without unnecessary additives).

Instructions:
1. Preheat the oven to 125 C / 250 F. Peel the butternut squash and slice thinly on a mandolin. If you are using a knife, make sure the slices are no more than 1/8 inch (1/4 cm) thin. Place in a bowl.
2. In a small bowl, mix melted coconut oil, gingerbread spice mix and stevia. Note: Butternut squash is naturally sweet and you may not need to use any sweetener.

3. Pour the oil mixture over the butternut squash and mix well to allow it everywhere.

4. Arrange the slices close to each other on a baking tray lined with parchment paper or a rack or an oven chip tray (you will need at least 2 of them).

5. Place in the oven and cook for about 1.5 hour or until crispy (the exact time depends on how thick the chips are).

Note: Half way through, you can spray them with a bit of coconut oil to help them crisp up.

6. Although the chips shouldn't burn at low temperature, you should keep an eye on them. When done, let them cool down and store in an air-tight container for up to a week.

Source: http://ketodietapp.com/Blog/post/2013/10/17/Chips-Crisps-Spiced-Butternut-Chips

Gummi Orange Slices- No Sugar High

Ingredients
• 1 T. vanilla extract
• ½ t. natural orange flavor
• Pinch real salt
• 1 ½ t. liquid stevia (every brand varies in sweetness, so add this 'to taste')
• 8 T. grassfed gelatin
• 1 can coconut milk
• 1 ½ C. water
• Natural orange food coloring to desired color
• Orange ice cube tray molds

Instructions:
1. Heat water and coconut milk over low heat until simmering.
2. Continue on low heat, slowly adding in each tablespoon of gelatin, whisking the entire time.
3. Add remaining ingredients and whisk until any clumps of gelatin are gone.
4. Pour into molds, and pour remaining liquid into 8X8 glass pan.
5. Put in fridge until solid. Gummis should pop out easily once hardened.

Source: http://mindfulmama.org/2013/10/16/gummi-orange-slices-no-sugar-high/

Jalapeño Paleo Pumpkin Seeds

Ingredients
• 1 1/2 cups pumpkin seeds, cleaned & dried
• 3 jalapeño peppers, sliced
• 3 tablespoons olive oil
• Sea salt and paprika, to taste

Directions
1. Prep Work: Once you've removed the seeds from the pumpkin, sorted pumpkin guts from pumpkin seeds, rinsed the seeds under cold running water, patted dry the seeds with a paper towel and transfered to a rimmed baking sheet to dry overnight or 24 hours – you should have dry-ish seeds, and you're ready to begin.
2. Preheat the oven to 350°F
3. If you haven't already, spread pumpkin seeds out on a rimmed baking sheet.
4. Add olive oil and sea salt and stir pumpkin seeds with your hands to combine.
5. Lay slices of jalapeño peppers on top of seeds.
6. Sprinkle paprika over the top of everything, generously.
7. Bake for 10 minutes.
8. Use a spatula to move the seeds and peppers around. Bake for another 5 minutes.
9. Move mixture around some more and bake for a final 5 minutes.
10. Remove tray from oven and let everything rest for 15-30 minutes to let the jalapeño-ness soak into the seeds.
11. Store in an airtight container…if you don't finish them all in one sitting.

Source: http://paleoporn.net/jalapeno-paleo-pumpkin-seeds/

Italian-Style Zucchini Rolls

Ingredients (makes 4 servings, 24-28 wraps):
• 3 small or baby zucchini, organic (210g / 7.4 oz)
• 14 thin slices streaky bacon (175g / 6.2 oz)
• 1 cup goat cheese, soft (200g / 7.1 oz)
• ½ cup sun-dried tomatoes, drained (55g / 1.9 oz)
• 4 tbsp raspberry vinegar or any other fruit vinegar, see recipe for my Homemade Fruit Vinegar. You can also use any sugar-free fruit vinegar like Star's Red Raspberry Vinegar or balsamic vinegar.
• ½ cup fresh basil

Notes: According to EWG's report, zucchini is on the list of 12 most contaminated with pesticides of fruits and vegetables. My advise: get them organic! When looking for ingredients, try to get them in their most natural form (organic, without unnecessary additives).

Instructions:
1. Preheat the oven to 200 C / 400 F. Using a peeler, slice the zucchini into thin stripes.
2. Place in a bowl and add the vinegar. Make sure you cover the zucchini from all sides. Leave to rest for 10 minutes.
3. Cut the bacon lengthwise and place on a rack or a baking tray lined with parchment paper. Bake until slightly crispy (but still soft) for about 5 minutes. Remove from the oven and place a bacon stripe onto each zucchini slice. Top with soft goat cheese, a small piece of sun-dried tomato and freshly chopped basil.
Note: Use drained, chopped sun-dried tomatoes marinated in oil. In most cases, the oil used is a mixture of sunflower and olive oil. I wouldn't recommend using it, as sunflower oil used in such product is almost certainly processed.
4. Wrap the zucchini rolls and pierce each one of them with a toothpick.

Source: http://ketodietapp.com/Blog/post/2013/10/14/Italian-Style-Zucchini-Rolls

Copycat Chocolate-Frosted Hostess Donuts

Ingredients:
For the donuts:
• 5 medjool dates, pitted
• 1 tbsp water, separated into 1/2 tablespoons
• 3 eggs
• 1 tsp vanilla
• 1/4 cup coconut flour
• 1/4 cup coconut oil, melted
• 1 tbsp cinnamon
• 1/4 tsp baking soda
• salt to taste

For the frosting:
• 1/2 cup Enjoy Life Chocolate Chips
• 1 tbsp coconut oil

Directions:
1. Turn on donut hole maker (You could also make these into regular donuts and cook at 350 for about 15 or so minutes).
2. Combine dates with 1/2 tbsp of water and heat in microwave for about 30 seconds.
3. Remove and add the other 1/2 tbsp and mash together to create a paste.
4. Combine date paste, eggs, and vanilla in a food processor until well combined.
5. Add in the rest of the ingredients and continue to process until all ingredients are incorporated.
6. Add appropriate amount of batter to donut hole maker and use as instructed (Mine took about 3 or so minutes for each batch, but this will vary for different types).
7. While your donuts are baking, prepare the frosting by combing chocolate chips and coconut oil over LOW heat until melted.
8. Once donuts are completely cooled, dip each in frosting with a toothpick or skewer and completely cover, tapping off excess frosting. (I used a longer skewer stick and placed them standing up in a cup to harden, but if you aren't concerned with appearance, you can dip them with a fork or spoon, even, and just place them on a plate).
9. Place donuts in refrigerator to completely harden (about 1 hour).

Source: http://taylormadeitpaleo.com/2013/07/17/copycat-chocolate-frosted-hostess-donuts/

Paleo Bacon Blue Cheese Spin Dip

Ingredients
• 3 slices bacon
• 3 oz blue cheese
• 2 large handfuls baby spinach, about 2 cups
• 1 can artichoke hearts, drained (reserve 1/2 tbls)
• 1/2 cup cashews
• 1 1/2 tbls olive oil
• 1/2 tbls artichoke juice
• 1/2 tsp onion powder
• 1/2 tsp garlic powder
• 1/4 tsp dry mustard
• salt and pepper to taste

Directions
1. Crisp bacon in a skillet over medium heat. Remove from heat and set aside on paper towels. Cut artichoke hearts in half lengthwise. In same skillet, warm artichoke hearts and sauté spinach. Let mixture cool. In blender, mix cashews until a fine powder. Drizzle in olive oil and reserved artichoke juice. Add in seasoning and half of artichoke spinach mixture. Pulse a couple times to combine but not liquify. In bowl, stir together blender ingredients, remaining spinach and artichoke, chopped bacon and crumbled blue cheese. Serve with sweet potato chips.

Source: http://www.plaidandpaleo.com/2013/10/paleo-bacon-blue-cheese-spin-dip.html

A bacon-ish, jerky-ish eggplant snack

Ingredients
• 1 large eggplant (about 1 pound)
• 1/2 cup olive oil
• 4 tablespoons balsamic vinegar
• 2 tablespoons pure maple syrup
• 1/2 teaspoon paprika
• Regular or applewood-smoked salt

Instructions
1. Wash eggplant and slice into thin strips. For ease in snacking you can cut long strips in half crosswise. Leave full-length for a more bacon-like appearance.
2. In a large bowl whisk together oil, vinegar, maple syrup, and paprika. Place strips in the mixture a few at a time, turning to make sure each is completely coated. If you run short of marinade, add a little more oil and stir it in with your hands.
3. Marinate 2 hours. Then, place strips on baking sheets or dehydrator trays as follows:
4. To dry in the oven: Line one or two rimmed baking sheets with parchment paper. Lay strips on sheets, close together but not overlapping. Sprinkle on a little salt (you don't need much). Place in oven on lowest setting for 10 to 12 hours (ovens' lowest setting varies, thus drying time will vary) or until dry and fairly crisp, turning strips partway through. Check occasionally, and if any oil pools on the sheets, blot with a paper towel.
5. To dry in a food dehydrator: Lay strips on mesh trays. While you do this, place a tray fitted with a solid sheet underneath the mesh tray to catch any

drips. Strips should be close but not overlapping. Sprinkle on a little salt (again, you don't need much). Place trays in dehydrator. Some oil may drip off during dehydrating, so place the tray with the solid sheet (you could use the one used earlier to catch drips of marinade) underneath the mesh trays holding the strips, and lay a couple of paper towels on the sheet. Dehydrate at 115°F for 12 to 18 hours or until dry and fairly crisp.

6. Store strips in an airtight container or plastic bag. Place a paper towel under or around strips to absorb any excess oil.

Source: http://everyoneeatsright.com/2013/10/08/eggplant-jerky-recipe/

Cheesy BLT Bites

Ingredients:
- 20 cherry tomatoes
- 8 pieces of bacon, cooked and crumbled
- 1/2 cup cream cheese (full-fat)
- 2 tbsp finely chopped spinach
- 1 1/2 tbsp grated parmesan cheese
- dash of sea salt

Directions:
1. Cut the top of each tomato off (just a small slice).
2. Scoop out the pulp and seeds and set aside. You can discard or use for making salsa, pasta sauce etc. I used my 1/4tsp measuring cup to easily scoop out the pulp. A regular spoon was much too big for the job.
3. In a bowl, combine the remaining ingredients and mix. Spoon filling into each tomato (I again used my 1/4 tsp measuring cup). To crumble the bacon I placed the cooked strips in unbleached parchment paper and crumpled it with my hand. Keep refrigerated, serve and enjoy!

Source: http://rethinksimple.com/recipes/cheesy-blt-bites/

Vanilla Pumpkin Seed Clusters

Ingredients
• 115g (1/2 cup) pumpkin seeds
• 1 tsp vanilla extract
• 2 tsp honey
• 2 tsp coconut sugar
• Water (boiled)

Instructions
1. Preheat oven to 150c.
2. In a medium bowl, combine the honey, coconut sugar and vanilla. Stir together to create a thick paste then add a small drop of boiled water to thin it out and create a runny syrup.
3. Pour in the pumpkin seeds and stir them around in the mixture to evenly coat them.
4. Dollop a generous tsp full of the pumpkin seeds onto a baking sheet, repeat until it's all used up and cook for 15-20 minutes until most of the seeds have browned (but don't let them burn!)
5. Take out of the oven and leave to cool for a few minutes. Once they've cooled a little (but are still warm) you can press the clusters together to make sure they don't fall apart. They will dry quickly.
6. Once they're cooled and dried, they're ready to eat! Enjoy on their own or served on top of your cereal.

Source: http://wallflowergirl.co.uk/vanilla-pumpkin-seed-clusters/

Maple Roasted Parsnip Chips

Ingredients
• 500g (1.1 pounds) Parsnips
• 1/4 Cup Coconut Oil, Melted
• 3 Tablespoons Maple Syrup

Instructions
1. Preheat the oven to 200°C (392°F) and get out an oven proof dish.
2. Peel the parsnips and cut them into chip sized pieces and place into the oven proof dish.
3. Pour over the coconut oil and distribute evenly.
4. Drizzle over the maple syrup and stir to combine well.
5. Place in the oven and cook for 15 minutes.
6. Remove from the oven and toss the parsnips over to allow the other side to brown.
7. Place back in the oven and cook for a further 10 to 15 minutes or until golden.
8. Remove from the oven and allow to cool a little before serving to the family.

Source: http://www.yummyinspirations.net/2013/08/maple-roasted-parsnip-chips/#sthash.NtxH3dMx.dpbs

Paleo Rosemary and Sea Salt Sweet Potato Chips

Ingredients
• 2 large sweet potatoes
• 1 Tbls coconut oil, melted
• 1 tsp sea salt
• 2 tsp dried rosemary

Directions
1. Heat oven to 375 degrees. The high heat will help crisp the chips. Peel sweet potatoes and slice using a mandolin set to 1/8th inch. Grind sea salt and rosemary with a mortar and pest. Toss sweet potatoes in a bowl with coconut oil and salt-seasoning mixture. Place on a non-stick baking sheet (or a regular pan greased with coconut oil) and place into the oven. After 10 minutes, take the pan out and flip the chips. Place chips back in for another 10 minutes. Pull the pan out and place any chips that are starting to brown on a cooling rack. Place the chips back in for 3-5 minutes. Every oven is different so keep a close eye on the chips so they don't burn. Place remaining chips on the cooling rack.

Source: http://www.plaidandpaleo.com/2013/07/paleo-rosemary-and-sea-salt-sweet.html

Raw Hemp Algae Bars

Ingredients
• 1/2 cup pistachios
• 1/2 cup pumpkin seeds
• 3/4 cup shredded coconut
• 1/4 cup orange juice
• 1/4 cup hemp seeds
• 1/4 cup coconut oil, melted
• 1/2 tsp spirulina
• 3/4 cup dates, chopped

Instructions
1. In a food processor, process the pistachios, pumpkin seeds, shredded coconut and dates until the mixture is crumbly but beginning to come together.
2. Remove to a medium mixing bowl and stir in orange juice, coconut oil, hemp seeds and spirulina.
3. Press into an 8-inch square cake pan or glass dish.

4. Chill in the refrigerator for at least an hour, then slice and serve.

Source: http://grokgrub.com/2013/08/02/recipe-raw-hemp-algae-bars/

Denali Trail Mix

Ingredients
• 1 cup flaked unsweetened coconut
• 1 cup raisins or dried cranberries
• 1/2 cup raw almonds
• 1/2 cup raw pecans or walnuts
• 1/2 cup raw pumpkin seeds
• 1/2 cup raw sunflower seeds
• 1/2 cup Enjoy Life Mini Chocolate Chips

Instructions
1. Combine all ingredients in a large mixing bowl and toss to combine.
2. Divide the trail mix between 9 sandwich baggies (about 1/2 cup of mix per bag) for a handy grab and go snack.

Source: http://www.allergyfreealaska.com/2013/09/16/denali-trail-mix-mt-mckinley-bears-gone-wild/

Healthy Fruit Leather (a.k.a roll ups)
Makes 10 strips

Ingredients
- 2 apples, finely diced
- 10 strawberries, diced
- 1 ruby pink grapefruit, diced
- Stevia/rice malt syrup to sweeten if needed
- 1 tsp cinnamon
- Pinch salt
- 1/4 cup water

Instructions
1. Place the fruit in saucepan with the water and bring to a boil. Reduce the heat and simmer until the fruit is soft and the liquid has been reduced. Stir through the cinnamon and salt.
2. Transfer the fruit to a blender and puree until smooth. Taste the mixture and if required add a sweetener. The grapefruit can be quite tart and while suitable for adults children may not appreciate this. If you would like a sweeter roll up than I suggest adding some sweetness to balance out the sourness. If a sweetener is added blend again until combined. You should end up with 2-3 cups worth of pureed fruit.
3. Heat oven to 120-150°C (250-300F). Line a large baking tray with baking paper (if your baking tray is not very large you may need to use two smaller sized trays). Pour the mixture onto the tray and spread it out thinly by using the back of a spatula. You want it to just cover the baking paper's surface without leaving any gaps (the thinner the better!). Place the baking tray in the oven on the lowest shelf available and bake for 8-12 hours. I left mine overnight baking at about 130°C for 9 hours. Remove the tray from the oven and using a sharp knife cut the fruit leather into strips. Let it cool completely before peeling the fruit leather off the baking paper. Roll up if desired and store in an airtight container for up to a week! Enjoy :)

Source: http://www.brookes-kitchen.com/2013/08/healthy-fruit-leather-aka-rollups.html

No-Ritos

Ingredients
• 3/4 cup almond flour
• 1/4 cup coconut flour
• 1/4 cup flax seeds
• 1/4 cup of butter
• 1/2 tsp salt
• 1 1/2 tsp chilli
• 1/2 tsp cumin
• 1/2 tsp paprika powder
• 1 egg
• 1/2 tsp garlic powder

Instructions
1. Melt the butter and basically mix up all the ingredients together, and knead it into a ball. Take 2 sheets of baking paper, lay the ball on one, the other sheet on top and then flatten it out with a roller.
2. Cut triangles with a knife. Heat the oven to about 180C (350F) and bake for about 10 mins. Keep an eye on them so they don't burn. Turn the oven off and let them harden for about another 15 mins.

Source: http://www.cavefoodkitchen.com/2013/09/no-ritos.html#.Ux_rQD-Swuc

Quick Crackers

Ingredients
• 1 heaped cup of almond meal
• 1 egg
• 20 grams finely chopped butter
• Pinch of salt

Instructions
1. Preheat your oven to 180 degrees Celsius or 350 degrees Fahrenheit.
2. Place your ingredients into your blender or food processor in the order listed above, quickly combine at medium speed – you don't want the mixture to become sticky or turn to almond butter, although do not worry if this happens, it will still work.
3. Roll the mixture into a ball and place between two sheets of baking paper, roll out to your desired thickness.

4. Remove the top layer of baking paper and place on an oven tray. Bake for 20 minutes or until nicely golden. Remove from the oven and allow to cool prior to cutting into crackers. Enjoy.

5. If you are using a thermomix I typically do 1 second at speed 6 and 15 grams of butter if using the thermomix scales.

Source: http://www.wholefoodsimply.com/quick-crackers/

Apple Peach Fig Bars

Ingredients
• 6 Eggs
• 2 tbs (30mL) Honey
• 1 tbs (15 mL) Coconut Oil
• 1/2 tsp (2.5 mL) Vanilla Extract
• 1/3 cup (40 g) Coconut Flour
• 1/4 tsp (1.25 mL) Baking Soda, optional
• 1/4 tsp (1.25 mL) Salt
• 2 tbs (30 mL) Applesauce
• 1/2 Peach, diced
• 1/2 Apple, diced
• 2 Figs, diced
• 1/8 tsp (1 mL) Nutmeg
• 1/8 tsp (1 mL) Ginger
• 1/4 tsp (1.25 mL) Cinnamon

Instructions
1. Preheat your oven to 325° F (163° C).
2. Grease an 8x8 inch pan (20x20 cm square) and line it with parchment paper.
3. Puree the eggs, honey, coconut oil, applesauce, and vanilla in a food processor or blender.
4. Add the coconut flour, baking soda, salt, and spices and blend until smooth.
5. Fold in the apple, peach, and figs.
6. Pour the batter into the prepared pan and bake for 35-40 min or until a toothpick inserted into the center comes out clean.
Note: This doubles nicely, so if you need more bars, just double everything in the recipe and use a 9x13 inch pan (22x33 cm rectangular pan) instead and increase the cooking time by approximately 5 minutes (I found 45 minutes works nicely).
Source: http://nourishedapp.com/blog/2013/8/29/figbars

Caveman Style Fries

Ingredients:
- Jicama, 2lb
- ½ c. + 1 tsp. unrefined coconut oil, melted
- ½ tsp. Sea Salt
- ¼ - ½ c. onion, diced (I like sweet onions)
- ¾ c. raw and/or grass-fed cheddar cheese, shredded (optional)
- Simple "Special" Sauce (combine ingredients below)
- ½ c. mayonnaise
- ¼ c. ketchup

Preparation:
1. Prepare your Simple "Special" Sauce by combining mayo & ketchup in a small bowl, stirring until blended well then refrigerate
2. Pre-heat oven to 400F and line baking sheet with foil
3. Skin and slice jicama into sticks (I used my handy dandy fry slicer)
4. Rinse the jicama and gently pat dry (they can remain damp…no biggy) and place into medium-large glass bowl
5. Evenly cover the jicama with the ½ c. melted coconut oil
6. Transfer the jicama onto the sheet and spread out, doing your best to shake off any excess oil
7. Sprinkle with sea salt
8. Place sheet into oven and bake for approx. 40 min (or until it reaches your desired texture) moving around occasionally so they brown evenly
9. Remove fries from the oven and carefully try to remove the excess coconut oil
10. Gather the fries together, so they're not spread on the sheet any longer and top with shredded cheese, place back in oven for 5 minutes allowing the cheese to melt
11. Prepare the grilled onions by sautéing the chopped onions in 1 tsp. coconut oil, cooking until a deep brown
12. Remove fries from the oven and finish assembling by topping with the grilled onions and a generous amount of Simple "Special" Sauce

Source: http://www.nummyformytummy.com/2013/08/caveman-style-fries.html

Power Snack

Ingredients:
- 1/2 Avocado
- 1/3 Cup Greek Yogurt
- 1/2 tsp Paprika
- 1/2 tsp Salt
- 1/2 tsp Garlic Powder

Instructions
Place the yogurt in the empty pit part of the avocado half. Sprinkle with all the seasonings and enjoy.

Source: http://guiltfreefoodiecutie.com/2013/08/04/power-snack/

Fire Roasted Red Pepper Poppers

Ingredients
- 1 1/2 (or two small…mine were huge) Red Bell Peppers
- 6 strips of bacon (I like Applegate Farms)
- 1 small cooked chicken breast
- red pepper flakes
- salt and pepper

Instructions
1. Pre-heat oven to 375. Also, light your grill if you plan on roasting the peppers before baking. It's not really necessary but adds flavor.
2. Chop red bell pepper into large chunks about 1" thick boats. I got twelve pieces out of 1 1/2 bell peppers.
3. Drizzle the peppers with olive oil and add a dash of salt and pepper.
4. Lay pepper pieces on the grill and close the lid. Cook until slightly charred, about 8 minutes. (You can skip this step and just pop them in the oven raw if you want, they will just take longer).
5. Break your cooked chicken breast into 12 bite sized pieces. Separate each bacon slice lengthwise into two pieces.
6. When your peppers are done let them cool (I didn't wait 'cause I was hungry). Place the piece of chicken in the pepper boat and sprinkle with red pepper flakes. Wrap the strip of bacon around to hold it all together.
7. Repeat and place in a baking dish. Bake for approx 25 minutes or until the bacon is cooked. If your peppers were not pre-cooked it may take longer.

Note: This could also work starting with uncooked chicken, just make sure everything is cooked when you pull it out of the oven. I just had cooked chicken on hand so that's what I used.

Source:http://pencilsandpancakes.com/2013/09/08/game-day-east-fire-roasted-red-pepper-poppers/

Buffalo Chicken Stuffed Bell Peppers

Ingredients
• 3 T grass-fed butter
• 1 lb ground chicken
• 8oz sliced mushrooms
• 2 ribs chopped celery
• 1/3 cup crumbled bleu cheese
• Franks Red Hot (a few tablespoons maybe?)
• 2 T grass-fed sour cream or homemade mayo
• 2 T arrowroot/tapioca flour (optional)
• 4 bell peppers, tops removed and seeds/white membrane removed

Instructions
1. Heat up butter in large skillet and add ground chicken. Break up, and add sliced mushrooms. Cook over medium-high heat until mushrooms begin browning. Add celery and cook until just softened
2. Remove chicken mixture to a bowl (or allow your pan to cool down a little) and mix in the ble cheese and enough Franks to coat everything (or to taste). Mix in a little sour cream or mayo to give it a creamy texture, and sprinkle in the thickener if you decided to use it (it wasn't worth the effort of finding it in the cabinet to me, so I omitted it).
3. Spoon mixture into 4 bell peppers. I only had 3, so I put the remainder in a ramekin and baked that separately.
4. Bake at 350 for 25 minutes or until the peppers begin softening up.
5. Remove and allow to cool for a few moments. Poke a hole in the bottom of each of the peppers to drain off additional moisture if you didn't add the arrowroot/tapioca.
6. Dig in and enjoy!

Source:http://www.homeindisarray.com/2013/10/buffalo-chicken-stuffed-bell-peppers.html

Homemade Sour Watermelon Gummies

Ingredients
• 4 cups fresh watermelon, cut into chunks (or 2 cups juice)
• 6 tbl grass fed gelatin
• 1/2 cup freshly squeezed lemon juice
• Optional, depending on the sweetness / ripeness of your watermelon: 1/4 cup raw honey

Instructions
1. Add the fresh watermelon to a blender and liquefy.
2. Strain the blended watermelon through a fine mesh strainer, discarding the pulp - you should have about 2 cups of juice.
3. Skim the small amount of white foam from the top of the watermelon juice and discard.
4. Divide the juice: add half to a small saucepan and the other half to a bowl.
5. Add the grass fed gelatin to the juice in the bowl by sprinkling it over the surface. Let it sit for a few minutes so that it dissolves into the juice. It will solidify.
6. Gently heat the watermelon juice in the saucepan just to warm it - do not bring it to a boil or simmer.
7. Add the gelatin & juice mixture to the rest of the juice in the saucepan. Whisk or stir to combine until the liquid is smooth.
8. Add the raw honey and lemon juice; whisk until dissolved and combined.
9. Pour the gelatin mixture into molds or a refrigerator safe pan.
10. Chill until set, about 30 minutes and then either remove the gelatin from the mold or slice it into pieces.
11. Can be stored at room temperature, although they are great cold.

Source: http://meatified.com/healthy-sour-watermelon-gummies/

Fire Roasted Tomato, Green Chile and Corn Salsa

Ingredients
• 1 ear organic/non-GMO sweet summer corn
• 1 red onion, peeled and quartered
• 1/4 cup roasted hot New Mexico green chiles
• 6 large garlic cloves, still in skin
• 1/2 cup cilantro, chopped
• 1 qt cherry tomatoes

• salt, to taste

Instruction

1. First things first, fire up the grill. Using charcoal or wood adds a nice touch to this salsa but 1) it's hot; 2) the gas grill is so much easier; and 3) unless you are serving this salsa as a condiment to a grilled meat (nice way to serve it by the way), it's a waste of charcoal/wood. So, I used our trusty gas grill on this.

2. After getting the grill hot, place the garlic on a grill plate and place in the grill directly over the heat.

3. The garlic take a little more time than the rest of the veggies, so I like to do them first. Close the cover of the grill and let the garlic roast for 3 – 5 minutes. When the skins begin to darken, turn them over and continue to cook another 3 minutes.

4. Remove the garlic from the grill. This is what they look like when they are done.

5. Now, place the tomatoes and onion in the grill pan and the shucked corn on the grill directly over the flames. Roast the veggies until nicely charred.

6. While the veggies are roasting, peel the garlic.

7. Place the garlic in a food processor.

8. When the veggies are finished roasting on the grill, add the tomatoes to the food processor along with the roasted New Mexico chiles and salt

9. Pulse to form a chunky puree.

10. Pour into a mixing bowl.

11. Now, hand dice the onions. I like the onions chunkier, about the same size as the corn. So, this eliminates using the food processor for the onions because it will chop them to finely.

12. Add the onions to the puree, the corn and now the cilantro.

13. Stir to incorporate and adjust seasoning, as necessary.

14. Pour into a serving vessel surrounded by tortilla chips. Serve & enjoy. I ate 75% of these and was lucky enough to get a photo of them before they were gone. :o

Source:http://remcooks.com/2013/08/20/fire-roasted-tomato-green-chile-and-corn-salsa/

Chapter 7
How To Prepare Paleo Budget-Friendly Meals

Do you still think that you cannot afford to go on a Paleo diet because it is costly? It is time to give up such thinking. Here, you will discover how affordable the diet is with these Paleo budget-friendly meals.

Clear Your Pantry and Kitchen

One of the first things you need to do is to clear your pantry and kitchen of non-Paleo food ingredients. Following this, perform an inventory of the Paleo items in your kitchen and pantry.

This step will allow you at least two things:

1. Avoid the temptation of reverting to your old diet.
2. Identify food items or ingredients that you need to buy to prepare your Paleo meals.

Plan for Your Meals

It will be better for you, as a Paleo beginner, to plan for your meals. You can choose to come up with a daily, weekly, or monthly meal planner. Meal planning will make it easier for you to transition to the Paleo diet. It also helps in budgeting and creating your Paleo shopping list.

Perhaps the best way to transition is to benefit from the 7-day Paleo beginners plan. This plan includes a Paleo diet-shopping guide that lets you save money as you benefit from the plan. It is also important that you are aware of what food to consume and what to avoid.

For practical purposes, it may be more efficient to create a weekly Paleo diet plan. You can do this in two ways:

1. Avail the Paleo weekly planner online. Several sites offer the meal planner, which among other things, should include the following:

• Easy to prepare and Paleo budget-friendly recipes
• Weekly shopping or grocery list
• Money-back or satisfaction guarantee
• The ability to cancel your subscription anytime

2. Create your own weekly planner of Paleo budget-friendly meals.

How to Create Your Own Weekly Meal Planner

If you choose to create your own weekly Paleo meal planner, follow these:

• Get a piece of paper or pull up your notepad/word processor. The first will allow you to produce the hard copy of your planner immediately, while the second will enable you to come up with your soft copy that you can print later on.

• List the day of the week, or pull up a weekly calendar template from your word processor or from the web. In each day of the week, divide it into three meals- breakfast, lunch, and dinner. You may also include up to two snacks per day.

• Start your planner with your dinner. This will allow you to plan and save from the leftovers. Remember, too, that you can skip on eating your Paleo food for three meals weekly.

You have the freedom to choose how- whether you want to have a full day-off from your Paleo diet, or on a staggered basis, e.g. skipping Paleo breakfast on Monday, lunch on Wednesday, and dinner on Friday. It is up to you to come up with your cheat meal scheme.

• Your dinner can be your breakfast, too. This means that your breakfast should consist of food items similar to your dinner, instead of the usual bread and cereals. Use your dinner leftover to create a delicious breakfast meal.

Here is a sample weekly planner of Paleo budget-friendly meals:

Monday
Breakfast: Steak Salad (some ingredients from leftover of your Sunday dinner)
Lunch: Baked Salmon
Dinner: Salmon Green Salad
Snacks: Baked Sweet Potatoes, Bananas with Almond Butter

Tuesday
Breakfast: Egg Salad
Lunch: Coconut Chicken
Dinner: Pork Loin Chops
Snacks: Kale Chips, Unsalted Sunflower Seeds

Wednesday
Breakfast: Pork Loin Stir-Fry
Lunch: Chicken Waldorf Salad
Dinner: Baked Tuna
Snacks: Banana Smoothie

Thursday
Breakfast: Tuna Pancake
Lunch: Fish with Vegetable Curry
Dinner: Turkey Burgers
Snacks: Fruit Salad

Friday
Breakfast: Turkey Burger Wrap
Lunch: Egg Drop Soup and Chef Salad
Dinner: Grilled Chicken and Cauliflower Rice
Snacks: Dark chocolate, green smoothie

Saturday
Breakfast: Chicken Wrap
Lunch: Grilled Shrimp
Dinner: Beef Roast Pot
Snacks: Guacamole, Homemade Apple Chips

Sunday
Cheat Day
You can eat non-Paleo breakfast, lunch, and dinner meals

Sample Paleo Recipes

Here are some sample recipes friendly to your Paleo budget:

Recipe #1: Tuna-filled Pancake

Ingredients: a cup of almond flour, 1 tablespoon of coconut flour, 2 organic eggs, ¼ cup water, leftover tuna flakes, coconut oil, sea salt to taste (optional)

Procedure:

1. In a mixing bowl, combine the following ingredients: almond flour, coconut flour, eggs, water, and sea salt (optional). Mix the ingredients thoroughly until you are able to form a batter according to your desired consistency.

2. Use a non-stick pan to cook your pancake. Pour some coconut oil on the pan and then set your stove to medium-low heat. Meanwhile, combine your tuna flakes with the batter.

3. When the pan reaches desirable heat level, scoop your tuna batter and drop it onto the heated pan. Spread your batter if you wish. When you see bubbles forming on the pancake, flip it to cook the bottom side. When the sides start to brown or after a minute or two, remove the pancake and repeat this step for your remaining batter.

Recipe #2: Grilled Chicken and Cauliflower Rice

Ingredients: (Grilled Chicken) 2 pieces of boneless chicken breast, 3 tablespoons of olive oil (preferably extra virgin), 2 cloves of garlic (minced), a teaspoon of dried thyme, half a teaspoon of dried oregano, ½ teaspoon of lemon extract, ground black pepper and kosher salt to taste

(Cauliflower Rice) ½ to 1 head of cauliflower (medium-sized), finely chopped green onion, a dash of cayenne pepper, ground black pepper and kosher salt to taste, a tablespoon of olive or coconut oil

Procedure:

Grilled Chicken

1. Except for the chicken breast, mix the ingredients and then place the mixture in a zip-lock bag. Meanwhile, pound the chicken breast to flatten it with about half an inch thickness. Add the pounded chicken breast to the mixture.

2. Massage from the outside of the bag to ensure the even spread of the mixture into the chicken. Place the bag in a container before putting it inside your refrigerator to let it marinate for a minimum of four (4) hours or overnight.

3. When the chicken is ready, prepare to grill. Set the temperature to high and once heated; start to grill the marinated chicken breast.

Cauliflower Rice

1. Rinse the cauliflower thoroughly. Chop it into tiny pieces, or use a food processor/blender.

2. Heat the skillet with olive or coconut oil. Pour the chopped cauliflower into the skillet and let it cook over medium-high heat temperature until it becomes soft with rice-like consistency. Add your spices.

Now you are ready to enjoy the benefits of Paleo budget-friendly meals.

Chapter 8
Paleo Diet Shopping Guide

Are you ready to start benefitting from what could be your healthiest diet plan? If you are about to shift to the Paleo diet, it is necessary that you clean your kitchen and begin stocking up Paleo food items and ingredients. Use the information here as your practical Paleo diet shopping guide.

What Food to Eat

Before creating your shopping list, it is important that you know what food to eat under the Paleo diet plan. You can eat practically everything including modern food as long as they are healthy and wholesome.

You should consume these food items if you follow the Paleo diet:

• Meat from free-ranging or grass-fed animals
• Fish and seafood
• Fresh fruits and vegetables
• Seeds and nuts excluding peanuts
• Healthy oils, e.g. coconut, olive, almond, walnut, avocado, macadamia, and flaxseed

It also helps that you are aware of the food items that you should not consume, such as the following:

• Grains and cereals
• Legumes (beans, peanuts, lentils, and peas)
• Dairy and dairy products
• Refined sugar
• Refined oils
• Salt
• Processed food
• Potatoes

Preparing Your Meal Plan

It is relatively easy and simple to prepare a Paleo meal plan considering the resources readily available on the web. Preparing your meal plan is an essential element of your Paleo diet shopping guide.

You can create your own meal plan by following these guidelines:

• Consume loads of vegetables, and include fruits, too. Hence, your shopping list should consist mostly of fresh veggies and fruits.

• Use lean cuts of meat from free-ranging or grass-fed animals. Stay away from processed meat such as hotdogs.

• Be sure to include healthy fats in your meals. Contrary to common belief, including fats in your diet can actually help you lose excess weight or maintain your recommended weight.

• You can eat your bacon, but make sure it comes from organic or pastured sources. Avoid those that come from factory farming sources since they contain residues of toxic substances.

• Make sure that you vary your meals, and never be afraid to experiment.

As an example of a Paleo meal, look at the following:

Your plate should consist of about 6 oz. of lean meat cuts such as pork loin, chicken, seafood, or lean beef; generous servings of veggies (slightly cooked, steamed, or raw), and healthy fats (olive oil, coconut oil, or avocado oil) or snack with unsalted nuts (almond, macadamia, walnut, or pecan).

Create Your Shopping List

After creating your meal plan (daily, weekly, or monthly), the next thing to do is to perform an inventory of your kitchen and pantry. Make sure that you have decent supply of ingredients. Following this, it is time to create your shopping list.

Here is an example of a weekly grocery list:

Meat

• Lean beef
• Pork loin or ground pork
• Your preferred cut of chicken
• Your preferred cut of steak
• Your preferred fish meat /seafood
• Fresh organic eggs

Vegetables / Fruits

• Carrots
• Onions
• Garlic
• Tomatoes
• Broccoli
• Cucumber
• Mushroom
• Lemon
• Sweet potatoes
• Avocadoes (which you can consume as a fruit or as healthy oil)
• Other in-season veggies

Nuts and Seeds
• Your choice of nuts: almonds, macadamia, pecan, walnuts, brazil nuts, cashew, or pistachio
• Your choice of seeds: flaxseed, sesame, sunflower, or pumpkin

Healthy Oils
• Coconut oil and olive oil for multi-purpose cooking
• Flaxseed oil as Omega 3-supplement
• Your choice between avocado oil and walnut oil for your salad
• Sesame oil for cooking food requiring low heat

Beverages
• Coconut milk or water
• Water
• Almond milk
• Green tea or your choice of herbal tea

Sweets
• Dark chocolate
• Natural sweetener
• Raw honey

Here are some tips when buying your Paleo items o ingredients:

• In buying fruits, choose those with low fructose such as the following: berries, apples, cherries, grapefruit, apricots, figs, and peaches. These fruits are safe for daily consumption.

• Remember that not all veggies you may consume. This Paleo diet shopping guide recommends that you create the list of food items that you should not eat.

Examples of non-Paleo vegetables are potatoes and corns, the former for its nutritional deficiencies and the latter because they are grains.

• Avoid buying factory-farmed meat. If you are having difficulty buying organic, pastured, or grass-fed meat from your local grocery, get them online from reputable sellers.

• For each of your weekly grocery list, include a new Paleo item. For instance, choose a vegetable that you do not normally eat or a fruit that is in-season.

• Bring your grocery list with you in order to avoid the temptation of buying non-Paleo items including processed and junk food. Follow your list strictly.

Where to Buy Your Paleo Food Items and Ingredients

When you are very much familiar with Paleo, you can shop anywhere to buy your Paleo food items and ingredients. With beginners, however, it is best that you choose stores, online or offline, which are Paleo-friendly.

Here are some good stores:

• Costco
• Trader Joes
• Whole Foods
• Rorabeck's Farmer's Market
• Liberty Heights Fresh

You may also want to consider online sellers that deliver Paleo meals, food items or ingredients such as high quality organic meat. Before choosing the site from where to purchase, be sure to check its legitimacy, reliability, and reputability.

Practical Tips

Paleo does not have to be expensive. In fact, if you are diligent in getting to know the diet plan, you will realize how economical your Paleo meals are. Here are some practical tips:

• If the best cuts of meat are costly to you, what you can do is to choose ruminant meat such as beef and lamb over pork and chicken.

• Avoid over-buying fresh fish and sea food. If you plan to stock up, choose the frozen variety.

• Consider buying organic eggs as an economical source of protein. For instance, you may want to use it as a substitute for your free-roaming chicken meat, wherever possible.

Preparation is the key to benefit much from the Paleo diet plan. Creating your shopping list is an essential element in preparing your Paleo diet. Always refer to this Paleo diet shopping guide to make sure that you are treading the right path.

Yap Kee Chong
8345 NW 66 ST #B7885
Miami, FL 33166

Copyright 2015

Get Notice of Our New Releases Here!
http://eepurl.com/7tcHf

Check Out Our Other Books

Self Help

ADHD Adult: How To Recognize & Cope With Adult ADHD In 30 Easy Steps

Conversation Skills: How To Talk To Anyone & Build Quick Rapport In 30 Steps

Ending Emotional Eating: Tips And Strategies To Stop Emotional Eating In 30 Days

House Cleaning Guide: 70+ Top Natural House Cleaning Hacks Exposed

Intuitive Eating: 30 Intuitive Eating Tips & Strategies For A Healthy Body & Mind Today!

Organized Mind: How To Excel In Math & Science In 30 Easy Steps

Organized Mind: How To Rewire Your Brain To Stop Bad Habits & Addiction In 30 Easy Steps

Organized Mind: How To Think Straight And Make All The Right Life Decisions In 30 Easy Steps

Stress Eating: How to Handle the Stress Triggers that Lead to Emotional Eating, Stress Eating and Binge Eating & Beat It Now!

Creative Confidence: How To Unleash Your Confidence & Easily Write 3000 Words Without Writer's Block Box Set

Creative Confidence: How To Unleash Your Confidence, Be Super Innovative & Design Your Life In 30 Days

Journaling: The Super Easy Five Minute Journaling Like A Pro Box Set

Journaling: The Super Easy Five Minute Basics To Journaling Like A Pro In 30 Days

397 Journaling Writing Prompts & Ideas: Your Secret Checklist To Journaling Like A Super Pro In Five Minutes

Habit Stacking: How To Set Smart Goals & Avoid Procrastination In 30 Easy Steps (Box Set)

Habit Stacking: Goal Setting: How To Set Smart Goals & Achieve All Of Them Now

Habit Stacking: How To Change Any Habit In 30 Days

Habit Stacking: How To Beat Procrastination In 30+ Easy Steps (The Power Habit Of A Go Getter)

Habit Stacking: How To Write 3000 Words & Avoid Writer's Block (The Power Habits Of A Great Writer)

Declutter Your Home Fast: Organization Ideas To Declutter & Organize Your Home In Just 15 Minutes A Day!

Emotional Vampires: How to Deal with Emotional Vampires & Break the Cycle of Manipulation. A Self Guide to Take Control of Your Life & Emotional Freedom

Memory Improvement: Techniques, Tricks & Exercises How To Train and Develop Your Brain In 30 Days

Mind Mapping: Step-By-Step Beginner's Guide In Creating Mind Maps!

Hobbies & Crafts

Doodling: How To Master Doodling In 6 Easy Steps

Making Costume Jewelry: An Easy & Complete Step By Step Guide
Paracord Bracelets & Projects: A Beginners Guide (Mastering Paracord Bracelets & Projects Now)

Jewelry Making For Beginners: A Complete & Easy Step by Step Guide
How To Make Jewelry With Beads: An Easy & Complete Step By Step Guide

Silver Jewelry Making: An Easy & Complete Step by Step Guide
Gaming & Entertainment

The Miner's Combat Handbook: 50+ Unofficial Minecraft Strategies For Combat Handbook Exposed

The Miner's Traps: 50+ Unofficial Minecraft Traps Exposed!

The Miner's XBOX 360 Handbook: 50+ Unofficial Minecraft XBOX 360 Tips & Tricks Exposed!

Miner's Kids Stories: Unofficial 2015 Box Set of 50+ Minecraft Short Stories, Jokes, Memes & More For Kids

Miner's Survival Handbook: Unofficial 2015 Box Set of Minecraft Cheats, Seeds, Redstone, Mods, House And More!

The Miner's Redstone 2015: Top Unofficial Minecraft Redstone Handbook Exposed!

The Miner's Seeds 2015: Top Unofficial Minecraft Seeds Tips & Tricks Handbook Exposed!

The Miner's Mod 2015 : Top Unofficial Minecraft Mods Tips & Tricks Handbook Exposed!

The Miner's Pocket Edition 2015: Top Unofficial Tips & Tricks Minecraft Handbook Exposed!

The Miner's Jokes For Kids : 50+ Unofficial Collection Of Minecraft Fun Jokes, Memes, Puns, Riddles & More!

The Miner's Craft 2015: Top Unofficial Minecraft Tips & Tricks Handbook Exposed!

The Miner's House 2015: Top Unofficial Minecraft House Tips & Handbook Exposed!

The Miner's A - Z Unofficial Compendium For Minecraft Combat Success
Kids Stories From The Miner: 50+ Unofficial Collection Of Fun Minecraft Stories Of Creepers, Skeleton & More For Kids

The Miner's Cheats 2015: Top Unofficial Minecraft Cheats Handbook Exposed!

Poker Strategy: How To Get The Unfair Winning Edge In Any Tournament. The Secret Strategies Of Poker Mega Stars Revealed!

Diet

10 Day Green Smoothie Cleanse: A Box Set of 100+ Recipes For A Healthier You Now!

10 Day Green Smoothie Cleanse: 50 New And Fat Burning Paleo Smoothie Recipes For Your Rapid Weight Loss Now

10 Day Green Smoothie Cleanse: 50 New Beauty Blast Recipes To A Sexy New You Now

10 Day Green Smoothie Cleanse: 50 New Cholesterol Crusher Recipes To Reduce Cholesterol The Natural Way

10 Day Green Smoothie Cleanse: 50 New Cholesterol Crusher Recipes To Reduce Cholesterol The Natural Way

10 Day Green Smoothie Cleanse: 50 New Sleep Helper Recipes Revealed! Get The Sleep You Deserved Now

Autoimmune Paleo Cookbook: Top 30 Autoimmune Paleo (AIP) Breakfast Recipes Revealed!

Dash Diet Plan: The Ultimate Dash Diet Cheat Sheet For Weight Loss

Dash Diet Recipes: Top DASH Diet Cookbook & Eating Plan For Weight Loss

Green Smoothie Weight Loss: 70 Green Smoothie Recipes For Diet, Quick Detox, Cleanse & To Lose Weight Now!

Paleo Diet For Beginners: Top 30 Paleo Snack Recipes Revealed!

Paleo Diet For Beginners: Top 40 Paleo Lunch Recipes Revealed!

Paleo Diet For Beginners: Top 30 Paleo Cookie Recipes Revealed!

Paleo Diet For Beginners: Top 30 Paleo Comfort Food Recipes Revealed!

Paleo Diet For Beginners: Top 30 Paleo Bread Recipes Revealed!

Paleo Diet For Beginners: 70 Top Paleo Diet For Athletes Exposed!

Paleo Diet For Beginners: Top 30 Paleo Pasta Recipes Revealed!

Paleo Diet For Beginners: Top 50 Paleo Smoothie Recipes Revealed!

Autoimmune Paleo Cookbook: Top 30 Autoimmune Paleo Recipes Revealed!

Paleo Diet For Beginners: A Box Set Of 100+ Gluten Free Recipes For A Healthier You Now!

Super Immunity Superfoods: Super Immunity Superfoods That Will Boost Your Body's Defences & Detox Your Body For Better Health Today!

The DASH Diet Box Set: A Collection of Dash Diet Recipes & Cheat Sheets Health

Borderline Personality Disorder: 30+ Secrets How To Take Back Your Life When Dealing With BPD (A Self Help Guide)

Ebola Outbreak Survival Guide 2015: 5 Key Things You Need To Know About The Ebola Pandemic & Top 3 Preppers Survival Techniques They Don't Want You To Know

Thyroid Diet: Thyroid Solution Diet & Natural Treatment Book For Thyroid Problems & Hypothyroidism Revealed!

Bipolar Disorder: Am I Bipolar? How Bipolar Quiz & Tests Reveal The Answers

Bipolar Diet: How To Create The Right Bipolar Diet & Nutrition Plan- 4 Easy Steps Reveal How!

Bipolar Type 2: Creating The RIGHT Bipolar Diet & Nutritional Plan

Bipolar 2: Bipolar Survival Guide For Bipolar Type II: Are You At Risk? 9 Simple Tips To Deal With Bipolar Type II Today

Bipolar Teen: Bipolar Survival Guide For Teens: Is Your Teen At Risk? 15 Ways To Help & Cope With Your Bipolar Teen Today

Bipolar Child: Bipolar Survival Guide For Children: 7 Strategies To Help Your Children Cope With Bipolar Today

Anxiety and Depression: Stop!-Top Secrets To Beating Depression & Coping With Anxiety... Revealed! - Exclusive Edition

Anxiety And Phobia Workbook: 7 Self Help Ways How You Can Cure Them Now

7 Top Anxiety Management Techniques: How You Can Stop Anxiety And Release Stress Today

Depression Help: Stop! – 5 Top Secrets To Create A Depression Free Life… Finally Revealed – Exclusive Edition

Anxiety Workbook: Top 10 Powerful Steps How To Stop Your Anxiety Now... - Exclusive Edition

Depression Cure: The Depression Cure Formula: 7 Steps To Beat Depression Naturally Now – Exclusive Edition

Depression Workbook: A Complete & Quick 10 Steps Program To Beat Depression Now

Depression Self Help: 7 Quick Techniques To Stop Depression Today!
Hormone Balance: How To Reclaim Hormone Balance, Sex Drive, Sleep & Lose Weight Now

Fitness

Kettlebell: How To Perform Simple High Level Kettlebell Sculpting Moves Top 30 Express Kettlebell Workout Revealed!

Strength Training Diet & Nutrition: 7 Key Things To Create The Right Strength Training Diet Plan For You

Strength Training Machine: How To Stay Motivated At Strength Training With & Without A Strength Training Machine

Strength Training For Seniors: An Easy & Complete Step By Step Guide For You

Strength Training For Runners: The Best Forms Of Weight Training For Runners

Strength Training For Beginners: A Start Up Guide To Getting In Shape Easily Now!

The Ultimate Body Weight Workout: 50+ Advanced Body Weight Strength Training Exercises Exposed (Book One)

The Ultimate Body Weight Workout: 50+ Body Weight Strength Training For Women

The Ultimate Body Weight Workout: Top 10 Essential Body Weight Strength Training Equipments You MUST Have NOW

The Ultimate Body Weight Workout: Transform Your Body Using Your Own Body Weight

Survival & Outdoors

Preppers Guide: The Essential Prepper's Guide Box Set

Preppers Guide: The Essential Prepper's Guide & Handbook For Survival!
Self-Sufficiency: A Complete Guide For Family's Preparedness And Survival!

Bushcraft: 101 Bushcraft Survival Skill Box Set

Bushcraft: The Ultimate Bushcraft 101 Guide To Survive In The Wilderness Like A Pro

Bushcraft: 7 Top Tips Of Bushcraft Skills For Beginners

Religion

Religion For Atheists: The Ultimate Atheist Guide & Manual On The Religion Without God

Finance

Bitcoin: The Ultimate A-Z Of Profitable Bitcoin Trading & Mining Guide Exposed!

Minimalist: How To Prepare & Control Your Minimalist Budget In 30 Days Or Less & Get More Money Out Of Life Now

Cooking & Recipes

Kids Recipes Book: 70 Of The Best Ever Lunch Recipes That All Kids Will Eat... Revealed!

Kids Recipes Book: 70 Of The Best Ever Dinner Recipes That All Kids Will Eat... Revealed!

Kids Recipes: 70 Of The Best Ever Big Book Of Recipes That All Kids Love... Revealed!

Kids Recipes Books: 70 Of The Best Ever Breakfast Recipes That All Kids Will Eat... Revealed!

Barbecue Cookbook: 70 Time Tested Barbecue Meat Recipes Revealed!
Vegetarian Cookbooks: 70 Complete Vegan Recipes For Her Weight Loss & Diet Guide... Revealed!

Vegan Cookbook: 70 Vegan Breakfast Diet For Her Weight Loss Book... Revealed!

Vegan Cookbooks: 70 Scrumptious Vegan Dinner Recipes For Her Weight Loss... Revealed!

Vegan Cookbooks: 70 Vegan Lunch Recipes & Vegan Diet For Her Weight Loss Guide Revealed!

Barbecue Cookbook: 140 Of The Best Ever Barbecue Meat & BBQ Fish Recipes Book… Revealed!

BBQ Recipe: 70 Of The Best Ever Barbecue Vegetarian Recipes... Revealed!

BBQ Cookbooks: Make Your Summer Go With A Bang! A Simple Guide To Barbecuing

Barbecue Recipes: 70 Of The Best Ever Barbecue Fish Recipes… Revealed!
BBQ Recipe Book: 70 Of The Best Ever Healthy Barbecue Recipes… Revealed!

Barbecue Cookbook: 140 Of The Best Ever Healthy Vegetarian Barbecue Recipes Book… Revealed!

Grain Free Cookbook: Top 30 Brain Healthy, Grain & Gluten Free Recipes Exposed!

Technology

Scrum – Ultimate Guide To Scrum Agile Essential Practices!
Raspberry Pi: Raspberry Pi Guide On Python & Projects Programming In Easy Steps

Languages

Learn Languages: How To Learn Any Language Fast In Just 168 Hours (7 Days)

Pets

Essential Oils For Cats: Essential Oil Recipes, Usage, And Safety For Your Cat

Sports

Golf Instruction: How To Break 90 Consistently In 3 Easy Steps